## HEY BROTHER

**Synopsis:** As the saying goes, you can't pick your family. At odds brothers, hard drinking financial planner Ben and grad student Issac, are cohabitating in Ben's beachside North Carolina home and it isn't going well. Adding fuel to their fire is Kris, an Asian-American grad student, who sets her eyes on both of them, forcing a love triangle neither is prepared to handle.

**Cast Size:** 2 Males, 1 Female

# Little Man

## a play by Bekah Brunstetter

## SONG USE NOTE

Licensees are solely responsible for obtaining formal written permission from copyright owners to use copyrighted songs in the performance of this play and are strongly cautioned to do so. Licensees are solely responsible and liable for all song clearances and shall indemnify the copyright owners of this play and their licensing company and agent, Original Works Publishing, against all costs, expenses, losses and liabilities that may arise from song usage.

LITTLE MAN was originally produced on October 17, 2014 by the Los Angeles New Court Theatre at the McCadden Theatre Center. The producer was Eddie Vona. It was directed by Kyle Hester.

The cast was as follows:

| | |
|---|---|
| HOWIE | Eddie Vona |
| ANDY | Brandon Bales |
| WENDY | Jordan Mann |
| JED | David Silavin |
| STEFANIE | Marianna Caldwell |
| MELISSA | Josie Adams McCoy |

# CHARACTERS

HOWIE, 28, short and successful

ANDY, 28, in a band, best friends with Howie, gay, a little overweight

JED, 29, a douchebag, married to Wendy

WENDY, 28, hot, a Mom

STEFANIE, 28, very tall, used to be quite large

MELISSA, 28, reunion planning committee

# LITTLE MAN

*(A hill top in Cafayate, Argentina. HOWIE, in cuffed pants, old shirt, slip on shoes, sits with his back to us, observing a beautiful sunset.*

*A pile of mail sits next to him.*

*He is toying with a diamond ring. It catches the sun. He gives it one last look, then tosses it impulsively into the distance.*

*He almost cries, almost laughs. Composes himself. Starts to sift through the pile of mail. Finds a blue and gold envelope. Opens it. Studies it.*

*Then: STEFANIE, in underwear, in her room, holding the same card / envelope. She reads it over and over.*

*She stands in front of her mirror, inspects herself.*

*STEFANIE tries on eleven dresses.*

*Then: WENDY, in her home. She looks tired but works hard to pretend that she's not. She TEARS into the envelope with glee. She inspects it, hands nearly shaking. She runs her fingers over raised glossed letters.*

*JED enters with spit-up cloth over his shoulder. WENDY hands it to him, overjoyed. He reads it, feigns excitement.*

*Then, they are Gone.*

*Only HOWIE remains.*

*HOWIE dials ANDY.*

*ANDY appears, in tight jeans, a flannel and a child's bday party hat. A guitar slung over his shoulder. He answers. Children scream in the background.)*

ANDY:  Andy Joseph's corporate office, how may I corporate you?

HOWIE:  Andy! It's me!

ANDY:  Andy can't come to the phone right now, he's really busy and famous but also really grounded, would you like to leave a message?

HOWIE:  Awwwwww. Tell him it's his friend is calling from across the world *just* to tell him he's pretty.

ANDY:  Where are you?

HOWIE:  Argentina! On a ranch!

ANDY:  I thought you were in Costa Rica or Guam or something? Where's Guam, is Guam a place?

HOWIE:  I was in the Dominican Republic, now I'm here.

ANDY:  *(with a bad accent, something like Spain:)* ARGENTINA!

HOWIE:  You've gotta come visit.
It's so beautiful, man, the sun's going down right now and the world is vast and like everything's in perspective and simple and nothing else exists.

*(Beat.)*

Nothing else exists.

ANDY:  ….Cool!

*(A weird moment in which there is nothing to say.)*

   How's Rachel?

HOWIE:  What?

ANDY:  Is Rachel there?

HOWIE:  No um - she's back in Seattle.

ANDY:  Is this really happening right now, are you really calling me? Like with your voice?

HOWIE:  What?

ANDY:  No, I just mean it's been a while since we've --

HOWIE:  Well phone calls're inefficient.

ANDY:  And my voice gives you feelings.

HOWIE:  We've emailed and stuff --

ANDY:  My phone barely rings anymore. It makes me sad. Last week my Mom TEXTED ME that Milo died. She literally texted me RIP MILO CAT GONE TO HEAVEN PLEASE COME BURY LOVE MOM.

HOWIE:  Milo DIED?

ANDY:  Milo dead. RIP Milo.

HOWIE:  What the fuck?

ANDY: The fuck is that Milo was like 27 years old and the dude passed on.

HOWIE: Geez. I'm sorry.

ANDY: I forgive you.

*(A kid SCREAMS in rage or perhaps delight.)*

HOWIE: Where're you?
Are those – children?

ANDY: No! I'm not playing a kids birthday party, not at all.

HOWIE: Are you sure? Cause it sounds like kids.

ANDY: It's my nephew, it's a family thing.
Hey did you know the wheels on the bus go round and round?

HOWIE: Naturally!

ANDY: Like all through the town.

HOWIE: How old is he now?

ANDY: He's turning five, Isn't that insane?

HOWIE: He was born like yesterday!

ANDY: I know he calls me Uncle Andy and I can actually like *feel* my lack of health insurance.

HOWIE: Meh. Who needs it?

ANDY:  Apparently everyone.

*(Beat.)*

   You still there?

HOWIE:  Yeah I'm here!

ANDY:  So what's up?

HOWIE:  Just saying hi.

ANDY:  Yeah?

HOWIE:  Yeah!

ANDY:  ….Hi!

HOWIE:  Hi!

*(Beat.)*

   Hey, did you get the invitation? To the reunion?

ANDY:  Uh – yes – yes  I did – and then I think I lit it on
   fire a lot.

HOWIE:  You don't wanna go?

ANDY:  Wait, you *want* to?

HOWIE:  I mean – yeah, why not?

ANDY:  Because it's going to be horrible? Also I don't
   see the point in revisiting trauma.

HOWIE:  We weren't *traumatized.*

ANDY:  Oh, okay.

HOWIE:  *(laughing)* We weren't!

ANDY:  Are you being serious right now?

HOWIE:  How were we traumatized?

ANDY:  You're fucking with me, right?

HOWIE:  It was a weird time, but it's a weird time for everybody.

ANDY:  Yeah – 'weird time' –

HOWIE:  And either way, things're different now. *We* are different now.

ANDY:  Are we?

*(Beat.)*

HOWIE:  C'mon it'll be hilarious. And it's a good excuse to come home. I miss home.

HOWIE:  You're all over the world and you want to come *here?*

HOWIE:  We can get really high and go to Sears and try on pants -

ANDY:  Why do you want to do these things?

HOWIE:  Cause it'll be fun!

ANDY: For you. I can get high and go to Sears and try on pants whenever I want. I just chose not to.

*(Beat.)*

Wait that actually sounds like fun.

HOWIE: Right? And I want the food court. I want the food court to give me dysentery.

ANDY: Where's it at, where's the thing?

HOWIE: Back at school, there's a new gym or something—

ANDY: I'm absolutely not going there.

HOWIE: Pleeeeeeeaseeeee

ANDY: NO.

HOWIE: I'll buy you a doughnut.

*(Beat.)*

ANDY: Damnit.

HOWIE: C'mon, I don't wanna go alone.

ANDY: So don't go.

HOWIE: But I don't know, I want to.

ANDY: FINE. I'll go if you go. For like an hour. Tops. And you're buying my ticket. AND we're getting drunk after.

HOWIE: Done and done.
   Or maybe drunk before and also during.

ANDY: Yeah, all of the drunks.

HOWIE: Cool, so, I'll start looking at flights! Is there still an airport?

ANDY: Uh, yes, we have an airport, and it has a *Cinnabon*, so fuck you.

HOWIE: Wasn't the airport not getting enough traffic and was going to be a Target or a Bed Bath and Pottery Barn?

ANDY: It's still an airport.
   Geez, it's been forever since you've been back.

*(Beat.)*

   But I totally get why you've stayed away, I get that. I'm not trying to Crimes of the Heart you or anything.

HOWIE: I haven't stayed away.

*(Beat.)*

   I haven't done that, I haven't 'stayed away.'

*(Someone screams for ANDY.)*

ANDY: I'M ON A PHONE CALL HERE.

HOWIE: Do you really think that I've / stayed –

ANDY: Sorry – gotta go. Send me your flight stuff.

*(ANDY begrudgingly goes back to the party.*

*HOWIE stands, wiping dirt from his pants.*

*JED appears, towering a foot over him.*
*He just stands there, looking down at HOWIE.*

*Lights.*

*Then:*

*In the dark, a woman's voice through a microphone. She is not used to speaking through one. She is nervous, unaccustomed to public speaking, and is taking this super seriously.)*

VOICE: Hello? Hi! It's on. Wow, it's on. Okay.
Welcome, welcome! Welcome, Spartans! Class of 2004!
WOOOO!!!!!!!
*(Lackluster claps and cheers.)*
That's *right.* Spartans *ignite.* I'm Melissa Strong, and on behalf of the Class of 2004 reunion planning committee, I would like to welcome you to your Reunion!

*(Lackluster claps.)*

So - welcome! I already said that, but welcome.

*(Lights warm to include JED, STEFANIE, ANDY, WENDY and HOWIE, facing downstage, standing apart from each other, desperately clinging to drinks, listening to the announcer. They are all wearing humiliating nametags with their high school senior portraits in the corner. HOWIE's rocking a blazer, nice jeans, and moccasins. He looks nice. For a Little Man.*

*There is a large framed picture of a HANDSOME, ALL AMERICAN HIGH SCHOOL SENIOR stands center. He wears the tux of a high school senior portrait picture. This is KEN STRONG. He smiles.)*

Okay so! First off I'd like to thank my co-planning committee: Missy Lefeavers, Jessica McClure, Julien Patton, and um, I'm forgetting somebody, um –

*(WENDY dies. Smiles, self consciously.)*

…Wendy Love! Thanks so much you guys.

*(Weirdly, Wendy starts to clap for herself, because she thinks she's supposed to, but then she stops and beams awkwardly full of pride instead.)*

When you see any of these ladies tonight, give 'em some love because these ladies have worked really hard to give you guys a great night. Okay so, important information to relay to you right now. The coat check's the girl's locker room, and the boy's locker room is actually the unisex bathroom. And most IMPORTANTLY: Drinks. Woooo drinks! You should have received your two drink tickets with your nametag and welcome package. After that it's a cash bar. We *wanted* to do an open bar all night but unfortunately, as we all know too well, times are currently tough, financially speaking, amiright? Who's got buckets of student loans? Who's got three maxed out Amex's?! Raise those hands! Raise em up! What *What!*

*(All hands are raised with sheepish grins, except HOWIE.)*

Okay so also – yeah so the bar is towards the back, I think you've all already found it, so it's in the back. I said that. And the food is right next to the bar, catered by – *(shuffling)* by TJ's Deli! We all remember TJ's sandwiches and yummy chicken tenders and bangin' banana pudding from high school, and now here they are again, for us to enjoy! Great. Okay so, that's the food.

And so – okay so, activities! Wooo! Don't forget to sign the guestbook. And we'll be playing a slide show with tons of pictures of us during our golden years – I gotta say, I saw some pretty interesting outfits and hair-cuts when I was putting it together! Emily Perkins, I'm looking at YOU girl! Ha! So! And then we've got Karaoke set up by the door to the pool, and we'll be playing some really fun getting to know you games. And getting our DRANK on! So. And don't neglect the dance floor! I know some of you got some slick moves up your sleeves, even those Mom's and Dad's that never get out of the house! So.

*(More shuffling, and a pause.)*

Now before we uh – get this party started - we'd like to take a quick moment, I'd personally just – I wanted to have a moment of silence for our friend Ken Strong. It's um –

*(MELISSA takes a breath. Tries not to cry.)*

Sorry. I told myself I wouldn't cry. It's okay. I'm okay. Sorry.

*(Beat.)*

I can't believe it but it's been 7 years since he – passed away and I – I know he would've wanted to be here.

He probably woulda been up here WITH me totally dominating this speech right now and doing way better. And I know he's watching us right now. So I just – I thought we could take a moment and remember him. Okay, so.

*(A moment of remembrance that lasts a hair too long. Inside of this moment, everyone peeks at each other.)*

Okay so, thank you. There were other – oh sh -- we've lost a few other people too I – was supposed to say before – that silence was for them too.
Now if you'll all join me in singing the school song, that'd be awesome.

*(MUSIC starts. Nobody really knows the words.)*

*Come ye Spartans! Sing together,*
*Heart to heart and hand in hand.*
*Love and laughter long shall linger,*
*Echoing down these halls again.*
*Though the years may come between us,*
*Still our Spartan Spirit shines.*
*In our hearts you'll live forever Blue and Gold,*
*Mount Tabor High.*

MELISSA: Okay great. So now, um. Time to mingle!

*(Everyone disperses. HOWIE and ANDY remain, standing by KEN's portrait. They survey the crowd, uncomfortable.)*

ANDY: Bitch.

HOWIE: Who?

ANDY: Girl on the microphone. Melissa Sawyer. Ken's girlfriend. Was such a bitch.

HOWIE: Really?

ANDY: She told the lacrosse team that we had ovaries and that's why we spent all our time together.

HOWIE: I don't really remember her.
　　Did she used to have longer hair?

*(Someone passes by. HOWIE raises a glass.)*

HOWIE: Hey - how's it goin –

ANDY: Whaddup!

*(The person passes by. ANDY, mortified.)*

　　Ahhhhhhhh AWKWARD! This is so AWKWARD! I have no idea what to do with my limbs!

HOWIE: Just relax!

*(ANDY stands weirdly trying to look natural but just looks weird.)*

ANDY: Why're we *here*?

HOWIE: Because these are things that you do. This is a life thing that one does.

ANDY: But nobody *makes* you do stuff like this. It's not mandatory.

*(Beat.)*

There's like nobody here. Everybody and nobody and
we're the chodes who showed up.

*(Beat.)*

I was reading because of fuckbook nobody comes to
these anymore.

HOWIE:  All the more reason to be here.
I'm having fun.

ANDY:  No you're not. You're insane.

HOWIE:  I guess I'm nostalgic. I like old things.

ANDY:  Oh, he likes old things. Then let's go to Good-
will and see how many copies of *Kindergarden Cop* we
can find on VHS. C'mon.

HOWIE:  We're staying.

*(HOWIE drinks.)*

No one would even notice if we weren't here.
No one's talking to us.
I bet no one recognizes me.
I look really different.

*(Beat.)*

Do I look different?
I look different right?
Oh God please tell me I look different.

HOWIE:  You look different.

ANDY:  Great! Let's go!

HOWIE:  We've gotta stay for at least a little bit.

ANDY:  Why?

HOWIE:  Because we're here? Because we / flew down here and drove here and now we're here?

ANDY:  YOU flew down.
I have nothing to say to these people.
We don't know these people, who are they?
*(pointing)* Who is that? That person did NOT go to school here.

HOWIE:  Yeah they did, she was uh – in uh --

ANDY:  Nobody's talking to us.

HOWIE:  Well then let's talk to *them!*

*(But they don't move. ANDY exhales. Drinks.)*

ANDY:  *(of unrecognizable girl)* Oh wait she did go here? I think had sex with her.

HOWIE:  No you didn't.

ANDY:  Yes I did! On my drum set. Tenth grade.

HOWIE:  How do you have sex on a drumset?

ANDY:  It was like on and around and involving the drum set.

*(Beat.)*

21

I think it was having sex with *her* that made me realize
I was definitely into dudes.
I should thank her.

HOWIE:  I'm sure you'd make her night!

ANDY:  I'm not really gonna do that.
   I'm an asshole but only in my mind, not in real life.

HOWIE:  I know.

ANDY:  To being assholes but only in our minds.

*(They cheers.)*

   I'm glad it's just you and me though. I feel more safe.
   Safer-er.

HOWIE:  Yeah. Me too.

ANDY:  I mean it woulda been cool if Rachel was here
   but I don't mind that she couldn't make it, I'm glad it's
   just you and me.

HOWIE:  Me too.

*(HOWIE nods and checks his phone.*
*Beat. ANDY drinks.*
*HOWIE nods, ANDY drinks.*
*ANDY is uncomfortable, getting pissed.)*

   I am a musician, I am a professional musician.
   What the fuck is this, high school?!

HOWIE: Yep!

ANDY:  Why do I suddenly feel like I'm not wearing pants?

HOWIE:  You're wearing pants.

ANDY:  Sometimes I think I *feel* the nudity of Adam and Eve.
I don't even know if I believe that the Garden of Eden is a thing that actually happened and not just a brand of veggie burgers but sometimes just for a second I think I can feel their nudity. You know?

HOWIE:  *(no)* Yeah!

ANDY:  Great Conversation starter!
Going to pocket that – for later.

*(Beat.)*

Everything's exactly the same.
Everybody's like standing in the same groups.

HOWIE:  There's the new gym. The gym is new.
It's not – it's not *exactly* the same.
Everybody's changed in some way.

*(ANDY regards the picture of KEN.)*

ANDY:  Also are we in agreeance that this is weird? This giant Ken face?

HOWIE:  It's a memorial.

*(HOWIE drinks.)*

ANDY:  You can see it on the tree still too. The dent.
It's right off Hathaway.

HOWIE:  I haven't seen it.

*(Beat.)*

ANDY:  Is it weird for you?

HOWIE:  What?

ANDY:  That Ken's dead.

HOWIE:  It's not weird, it's sad.

ANDY:  How so?

HOWIE:  Because it's sad? When a person dies?

ANDY:  Yeah but you're probably not THAT sad.

HOWIE:  Of course I'm sad.

*(Beat.)*

    It was a long time ago.

*(Beat.)*

    How's your mom?

ANDY:  Good!

*(Beat.)*

    She's ah. She's fine.

*(Beat.)*

    I've been feeling kinda bad. For moving away.

HOWIE:  Just a half an hour away.

ANDY:  *(weirdly defensive)* Yeah, but I moved --

MELISSA (O.S.):  2 minutes til the game starts!!!!!!!!

ANDY:  OH MY GOD JED JENNINGS.

HOWIE:  Who? What?

ANDY:  Over. There.
    Stop looking!
    Look with like your eyes but not with your whole self!

HOWIE:  Okay – yeah – Jed –

ANDY:  Delicious asshole of my weird wet dreams. What
    the fuck is he doing here, he was a year older than us!

HOWIE:  I don't know.

ANDY:  Oh right, he married Wendy Love. Right there.
    Remember her? Also a bitch.
    They have a baby, there's something wrong with her, I
    can't remember –

HOWIE:  How do you know this?

ANDY:  *Facebook* man. You gotta get on it.

HOWIE:  Yeah, no thanks.

*(HOWIE checks his phone again.)*

ANDY:  What is that, why do you keep checking your
    phone?

HOWIE:  I'm not.

*(Beat.)*

ANDY:  Is it Rachel, or --?

HOWIE:  No.

*(Beat.)*

I put on offer on that ranch I was on. In Argentina.

ANDY:  Whoa –

HOWIE:  Just checking to see if I got it.

ANDY:  So you bought a ranch.

HOWIE:  *(weirdly proud)* Yeah, that's the plan.

ANDY:  So what, you're gonna like live there?

HOWIE:  That is also the plan.

ANDY:  How many plane tickets are you buying me to come visit?

HOWIE:  All of the plane tickets.

ANDY:  So how's it going to work, can you work from there?

HOWIE:  Yeah, maybe.

ANDY:  'maybe?'

HOWIE:  I uh, sold the company actually.

ANDY:  Really?

HOWIE:  Yeah.

*(A small smile grows across his face that HOWIE can't control.)*

ANDY:  …What? What's the smile?

HOWIE:  Nothing.

*(Beat.)*

    Sold it for five.

ANDY:  Thousand?

HOWIE:  Million.

ANDY:  WHAT?

HOWIE:  Shhhhh!

*(WENDY approaches. She's hot, wears a black dress and carries her second glass of wine, and a plate of chicken tenders with BBQ sauce.)*

WENDY:  Howie?!

HOWIE:  Hi - ?

WENDY:  Oh my God HOWIE!!!!! How're you???

*(She hugs him, almost knocking his drink out of his hand.)*

    You look so cute, look at you!
    Your nametag's wrong! It says Max!

HOWIE: No I've been going by my / middle name actually

WENDY: I totally remember you! *(Pointing to her nametag)* Wendy!

HOWIE: Wendy!

ANDY: *(so uncomfortable)* Heyyyyyyyyyyyy Wendy....

WENDY: Hi, how're you?
*(to HOWIE)* We had um, we had biology together sophomore year?

HOWIE: Wow, great memory!

ANDY: *(to Wendy)* We had freshman lit and one time I gave you a ride home and we went to Wendy's because your name is Wendy and also for the fries.

WENDY: *(I don't remember)* Right!

HOWIE: What's up, how are you?

WENDY: I was on the planning committee –

HOWIE: Oh yeah, I heard that! Thanks / for –

WENDY: Babies, I have a baby –

ANDY: *Nice!* What kind?

WENDY: What?

ANDY: Oh I mean boy or girl?

WENDY:  Oh I have an amazing little girl, Sophia. With a ph.

HOWIE:  Congrats!

WENDY:  This is my first night out in *forever,* I said to her, *Mommy's night out!* This kind of shitty glass of wine is *heaven* right now.

ANDY:  Cheers!

*(They cheers.)*

WENDY:  Isn't this so crazy?
We walked in and I was like Jed. Jed! Do you remember everybody?! All of the wine coolers we drank with these people? Some of these people?  I mean not everybody, I didn't hang out with like EVERYBODY.
Oh and I'm married, I married Jed –He's over – *(pointing)* there –

HOWIE:  Totally! I remember Jed, that's great!

WENDY:  Yeah so, we're married!

ANDY:  That's so great for you guys. When did you / guys

WENDY:  Five years, right after college!

ANDY:  Perfect!

WENDY:  What about you guys?

HOWIE:  Oh! I uh –

*(A LOUD ANNOUNCEMENT over microphone.)*

VOICE:   Hey guys it's me again! Okay so now we're gonna do a little fun getting to know you game thing and it's called *(shuffling)* Getting to Know You.

HOWIE:  Ha –

*(WENDY doesn't laugh.)*

VOICE:   Wait no that's the other – wooo! Chardonnay you guys, try the Chardonnay!

*(WENDY raises her glass.)*

WENDY:  WE LOVE YOU MELISSA!!! WOOO!!!!

VOICE:   This one is called: Two truths and One Lie.

WENDY:  I thought of this game, this game was my idea–

VOICE:   Okay so everybody you'll see a little color dot on the corner of your nametag. You have TWENTY SECONDS okay to find your group with the same color dot, and then find a corner, when I say go. And then once you're with your group you're going to go around the circle and everybody has to say two truths and one lie, and everybody gets to figure out what the lie is! Okay so – okay – GO!

*(WENDY shrieks, looks at her nametag, starts to spin around in circles a little bit. Mad scrambling. HOWIE looks at his nametag, sees a purple dot. Sees a purple dot on WENDY's as well.)*

WENDY:  Well, here we are!

ANDY: *(of all the scrambling)* What is happening?

HOWIE: It's a game –

ANDY: Am I supposed to be running?

WENDY: What color dot do you have?!

ANDY: I have a dot?

WENDY: *(looking at his nametag)* You have a gold dot – okay go find people with gold dots.

ANDY: I think I'll just stay here.

WENDY: But you're supposed / to –

*(STEFANIE, very tall but not large, approaches timidly.)*

STEFANIE: Hi purple dots –

WENDY: *(chanting)* Purple DOTS! Purple DOTS!

STEFANIE: Hey… Howie!

HOWIE: Stefanie?

STEFANIE: *(blushing)* Yeah! That's me!

HOWIE: I barely recognized you, wow –

STEFANIE: Ha, thanks…..

*(They hug.)*

STEFANIE: I thought it'd be like funny to like show up in a fake beard but totally pretend like I'm not wearing a fake beard, like it wasn't even on my face. But fortunately I slept on it.

HOWIE: The fake beard?

STEFANIE: The thought of the fake beard. I decided on this dress instead.

HOWIE: You look great. Great to see you! I'm going to stop saying Great.

STEFANIE: You too! You look great too.

ANDY: Andy.

STEFANIE: I remember, yeah. Hey!

*(She hugs him.)*

Hey Wendy –

WENDY: *(reading nametag)* Stefanie!
Wow you look / so

STEFANIE: Yeah, yeah –

*(Beat. The two can't figure out whether to hug or not.)*

We were in Drama club together.

WENDY: I was in drama club?

STEFANIE: For a minute.
Howie, wow, it's so good / to

*(JED approaches with a High Life. ANDY goes stiff. )*

ANDY:  YO.

JED:  What's up?

ANDY:  Andrew.

WENDY:  We can't be in the same group!! I messed up
   the tags, we're married!
   *(To everyone else)* I see him all the time anyways, he
   knows everything, we're married --

*(JED spots HOWIE.)*

JED:  *(ignoring WENDY)* LITTLE MAN!!!!!!!!

*(HOWIE goes stiff at this name.)*

JED:  How are you buddy?!

HOWIE:  I'm awesome man, how are you?

JED:  LITTLE MAN!!!!

*(JED re-enacts something really horrible and traumatic,
place his elbow on HOWIE's head like an arm rest.)*

   LITTLE MAN!!! Remember?

HOWIE:  Yeah! That was great!

JED:  We used to, me and Ken! We used to call you that!

ANDY:  And it was hilarious!

HOWIE:  Yeah, I remember!

*(JED goes to the portrait of Ken.)*

JED:  Buddy – you wouldn't believe who's here, LITTLE MAN!

*(He raises his beer to KEN, drinks.*
*WENDY laughs nervously, eats a chicken finger.)*

VOICE:  Okay so it looks like everyone's found their groups! Okay great. Good work. Okay so, now let's start with our truths and our lies! The object of the game is reveal information about your personal life, and introduce yourself to your old but also new friends. Okay so – Go!

*(ANDY, HOWIE, STEFANIE, WENDY and JED stare blankly at each other.)*

WENDY:  I'll go I'll go! *(She thinks.)* Okay so –I guess my first thing is that my little girl Sophia is my whole world….. Okay that's one. Two, um – I'm a part-time auditor for Novant Health but I'd rather just be home with Sophia all the time.

JED:  Wouldn't we all! Who wouldn't love that, to not go to work?

HOWIE:  I have a / home office

WENDY:  And three! Three! *(She thinks. Holds up her nearly gone glass of wine. Then, in a robot voice)* I. DO. NOT. LIKE. WHITE. WINE.

*(She laughs.)*

LIES!

JED: Honey, they were supposed to guess.

WENDY: Well I'm really bad at lying. So.

JED: That's not the game.

WENDY: I *KNOW.*

*(Beat.)*

HOWIE: What about you Jed?

JED: Uh, not much to know, I'm a salesman over at the Ford dealership –

ANDY: I thought you had that football scholarship, I recall a small parade?

JED: I got injured.

ANDY: Aww, tragedy --

JED: And then I had a business, I had a small business too, we were uh – we were selling sports bras with pockets, bra-ckets, but it didn't – (he trails off.) Tough time now to get a product of the ground.

ANDY: Tough luck, man.

JED: Let's see I uh – HUGE Giants fan – and uh --

WENDY: You love beer!

JED: Yep –

WENDY: You work too much!

JED: Ha! You're funny –

WENDY: You love your wife! You love Sophia!

*(Uncomfortable silence.)*

HOWIE: You hate the Giants, I gather?

*(JED nods.)*

HOWIE: Yeah! So! Andy I think you're next?

ANDY: Yes! Right. Tough act to follow. Two truths. One lie. I head a classic bluegrass band *Hang Low House,* www.hanglowhouse.com, we've got shows this winter in Boston, Chicago, New York, pretty much up and down the east coast, you can check out our tour dates online.

JED: You work at Starbucks, right?

ANDY: YEAH! Thank you. I almost forgot. Yes. I work at Starbucks. Yes I do.

HOWIE: He was gonna go to grad school in Chicago but he had to hang back and take care of his Mom, actually—

ANDY: *(self conscious)* Yeah, I did, so but that's just another -
Okay so that was one thing.
And let's see – I've recently been asked by *Disney* to submit some original music for an upcoming animated feature about Appalachia - In tenth grade Jed slammed me against a locker and called me a faggot, and I love mayonnaise.

WENDY:  That was four things –

ANDY:  Oops sorry, then I'll omit the thing I said about 'Jed and 'faggot.' Hate mayonnaise. It's like mayonnaise: why? Why spread savory cool whip all over a perfectly good sandwich?

*(Beat. All laugh awkwardly.)*

JED:  I was probably just kidding around.

ANDY:  It's cool no bigs it's, it's all good now it's whatever.
Howie's turn!

HOWIE:  Nah –

WENDY:  *(chanting)* How-ee! How-ee!

JED:  LITTLE MAN!!!

HOWIE:  Okay – I'll go – so – three things. Let's see, uh – three things. I – my favorite country to visit is Argentina, for the waterfalls. *(Murmurs of "wow" and "nice")* and um I live in Seattle now and *(Murmurs of "wow, wow that's far")* and uh, I'm really happy to be here. *(Beat.)* So.

STEFANIE:  So you're not happy to be here?

HOWIE:  What?

WENDY:  You don't live in Seattle?

HOWIE:  Oh – those're all true – I forgot the game, I forgot what we were doing –

STEFANIE: I'm in Seattle too!

HOWIE: No way! / That's

STEFANIE: Yeah just for like a year now.

JED: I couldn't handle that mess, all that rain.

WENDY: Awwwwww rain I hate rain –

HOWIE: That's just something we let everyone else believe so we can keep the city to ourselves. It's actually / pretty

JED: I could never live there.

*(Beat.)*

HOWIE: And you guy's're still here? I mean – you live --

JED: Yeah! We're here. Still.

ANDY: My buddy here is being modest. He's a millionaire.

*(HOWIE is instantly embarrassed.)*

HOWIE: Andy –

ANDY: What, isn't this what we're doing here?

HOWIE No –

ANDY: *(to group)* Just sold his company for ten million bucks.

STEFANIE: Seriously? That's --

HOWIE: *(so embarrassed)* Five. Yeah...pretty much, um—

JED: How're you a millionaire?

HOWIE: I own a small business? I started an / online -

JED: Are you not sure?

HOWIE: What?

JED: You said it like a question.

HOWIE: Oh, um. 'I own a small business.'

JED: So what kind of 'business' is it?

HOWIE: It's shoes actually –

JED: Shoes.

ANDY: It's so brilliant. Every time a person buys a pair of these shoes, a pair of them goes to a kid with no shoes in a third world country.

HOWIE: Yeah! So – that's what I do!

STEFANIE: I have a pair! That's you?

JED: How'd you get into that line of work?

HOWIE: Yeah I uh, after college I did some travelling with the Peace Corps, went to Argentina –

WENDY: For the waterfalls!!!

HOWIE:  Yes! And I wanted to get a full feel of the country, so I visited some of the poorer communities and – most of the kids didn't have shoes.

WENDY:  Oh My God. No *shoes?!*

HOWIE:  I know.

ANDY:  He is being modest STILL. He single handedly built this company from the ground UP, he's got like tons of awards for charitable business acts but like with more important names, he like INVENTED shoes-

HOWIE:  I didn't invent shoes.
Yeah so – that's going really well!

JED:  What kind of shoes are they?

*(HOWIE sticks out his foot.)*

WENDY:  *Cutteeeee!!!!!*

JED:  Huh – not really my style / but --

WENDY:  Do you make them for babies? Jed we should get Sophia a pair.

STEFANIE:  I have a pair! I totally have a pair of those, they're my whatever shoes!

HOWIE:  That's exactly what I wanted them to be!

*(HOWIE laughs awkwardly as ANDY drinks. A weird moment.)*

STEFANIE:  Okay so I'll go. Hiiiiiiiiii....I'm Stefanie.... I think I was 'Stef' in high school. I, um.

I manage a bakery in Seattle, it's called 'babycups,' we specialize in bite sized desserts –

HOWIE:  Babycups! I *love* babycups!!

STEFANIE:  No way, really?

HOWIE:  Yeah, my ex girlf – I LOVE that place.

ANDY:  Wait, ex?

HOWIE:  Yeah, we uh …yeah.

WENDY:  Okay so now, lie.

*(Beat.)*

STEFANIE:  I'm feeling really comfortable right now.

*(Beat.)*

WENDY:  Cheers you guys!!!

*(They cheers. They look around.)*

ANDY:  *(to Howie)*  When did you / guys –

HOWIE:  It's okay, we don't need to --

JED:   Looks like – everybody's else is still playing, I guess uh -

WENDY:  Favorite memory from high school!

ANDY:  Is this another game?

WENDY: Yes! I just invented it. New game. Favorite memory. Off the top of your head. Howie, go!

*(Everyone looks at HOWIE.)*

HOWIE: I – Uh.

ANDY: Come on How.

WENDY: Example: Spartan pride parade float 2002 or 2003 Jed was it 2002 or 2003 with the paper mache football player with the arm that actually moved? We built it out of lawnmower parts! IT WAS SO AWE-SOME!

JED: I don't know.

WENDY: That's mine.

HOWIE: Uh.

*(They all look at him blankly.)*

I had a – really great parking spot. Under a tree. We got assigned parking spots, I remember that, and – it was really fair. There was no – they just drew names from a hat. And I got the best spot. It had nothing to do with who you were. You were just a name in a hat.

JED: Oh yeah, Ken was so mad you got that spot, that drove him crazy! Ah man.

ANDY: Yep, that's probably why he pissed in How's car / among other things!

HOWIE: It's Max now. It's no big deal -

WENDY: Did he really? He didn't – really -

HOWIE: It was really close to the main building, underneath this Dogwood tree, tons of shade, and when I'd come out of class, in the Spring, the whole car'd be covered with white flowers. It was like a wedding but on my car.

*(Beat.)*

I just really liked that. How fair it was.

*(He drinks while everyone just looks at him.
MELISSA, over the intercom.)*

VOICE: Alright you guys! I hate to tear you away from your new BFF's but I gotta! Let's change groups! Everybody – no wait on the count of three everybody go find a buddy, but it has to be a person you weren't friends with in high school okay? Yeah let's bust up on this segregation that's happening – I don't mean segregation like *race* I just mean like –Okay so find a person, make some eye contact, you remember the buddy system, okay so – GO! MINGLE!

*(Again, a mad scrambling. WENDY squeals, points at someone, and runs off.
JED downs his beer.)*

JED: Millionaire.
   Way to go, Little Man.

*(He goes.
STEFANIE, pained, goes as well.)*

ANDY: Why didn't you tell me?

43

HOWIE:  What?

ANDY:  Uh, about Rachel?

HOWIE:  It's not exactly my favorite thing to say.

ANDY:  But you could've told me.

HOWIE:  I know.

ANDY:  What happened?

HOWIE:  Just, ah. She wasn't happy.  I'm fine.  It's just.
It's fine.

*(They just stand there.)*

ANDY:  You coulda called me.

HOWIE:  I know.

ANDY:  No, you don't know, because you never –

*(Again, they just stand there.)*

HOWIE:  It's – it's fine, we just, it didn't – we didn't –
you know.

ANDY:  No. I don't. When –

HOWIE:  Like three months ago?
I didn't wanna make a big deal about it.

*(They look out into the crowd.)*

ANDY:  Are you sure you're / okay

HOWIE: Yes.

ANDY: What did / she say

HOWIE: I don't know, I kind of don't want to talk / about it right now?

ANDY: Okay sorry –

HOWIE: It's okay. It's fine.

*(Beat.*
*A long moment in which the music seems to get louder, worse.)*

ANDY: She doesn't know what she's missing.

*(HOWIE smiles, drinks.)*

HOWIE: Yeah.

ANDY: *(pointing to HOWIE)* this guy.

HOWIE: Yeah, *this* guy.

*(They stand there together, disconnected.*
*ANDY points at someone we can't see.)*

HOWIE: What're you doing?

ANDY: I've just made eye contact.

HOWIE: With who?

*(ANDY downs his drink.)*

ANDY: That person. Over there. I'm goin in. I am JUST drunk enough to do this.

*(He looks at Howie.)*

ANDY: You *sure* you're okay?

HOWIE: I'm fine, could you just not –

ANDY: Fine. Sorry.

*(Then, to someone we can't see:)*

Hey buddy!

*(ANDY goes. HOWIE stands by himself, dying inside. Gets out his phone to text, or receive. Has nothing. Sends nothing. Sits in a folding chair.*

*Slowly, STEFANIE re-approaches him.)*

STEFANIE: Can I sit next to you for a minute? You look like a safe place. To sit.

HOWIE: Sure!

*(They sit next to each other, looking out.)*

STEFANIE: It's so satisfying. The ones who got fat.

HOWIE: To the fat ones!

*(They cheers.)*

STEFANIE: Nobody's playing the game right, nobody's really mingling.
We're like separated into groups.

HOWIE:  How so?

STEFANIE:  *(pointing)* People with babies and people with not babies.

HOWIE:  Huh.

STEFANIE:  *(pointing)* See over there are the people with babies being all *babies!!!*
And here we are.
Being barren.

HOWIE:  I'm not barren. Impotent. The man version.

STEFANIE:  Me neither, I'm fertile, very.

HOWIE:  I want kids, I think.

STEFANIE:  Like when?

HOWIE:  I don't know, soon?

STEFANIE:  Oh, but we just met.

HOWIE:  Um, you were the tuba to my trombone, I think we're pretty much life partners.

*(STEFANIE smiles.)*

STEFANIE:  Well I want to wait like just a little while. For kids. I want to really want them.

HOWIE:  Yeah let's wait. At least a few days.

STEFANIE:  Til I'm ovulating.

HOWIE:  I was / kidding

STEFANIE:  No me too I was kidding too I was so kidding.

*(Beat.)*

STEFANIE:  Sorry about your – ex – thing –

*(HOWIE shrugs. Drinks. Drinks more.)*

Is it a – pretty recent - ?

HOWIE:  Hey, you win some you lose some, it's all, you know, it's just part of life, people come and go, in and out of your life, and yeah.

*(Beat.)*

STEFANIE:  Favorite coffee in Seattle.

HOWIE:  Was that a question?

STEFANIE:  Yes! One two three GO / BEDLAM

HOWIE:  BEDLAM.

STEFANIE:  AHHHHHH BEDLAM!!!!

HOWIE:  Americano with just like a / *touch* of soy

STEFANIE:  TOUCH OF SOY and like the / TINIEST sprinkling of turbinado

HOWIE:  Turbinado!

*(Beat. They look at each other.)*

STEFANIE:  I want one. Right now. But I'll drink this vodka soda instead.

HOWIE:  Cheers.

STEFANIE:  Cheers.

*(She drinks, a lot. Still nervous, but a bit more relaxed. Again, they look out into the crowd.)*

HOWIE:  Can I ask / you

STEFANIE:  Yep!

HOWIE:  How'd you lose all the weight?

STEFANIE:  Oh.

HOWIE:  Sorry –

STEFANIE:  No, it's okay, I kinda like to talk about it. It's like the one thing I've ever really done.

HOWIE:  Uh, you have a bakery –

STEFANIE:  Right! I did that.

*(Beat.)*

I was just tired. Of being – it's crazy how much mental energy you can waste like – resenting who you are. Your body. And I wanted to make room in my other brain for things other than 'I am fat.' And then I realized I didn't need food. I got really into those very small wheels of cheese. I was like: all the food I used to eat? I don't need that food. I'll just eat this almond instead.

HOWIE:  You weren't / fat

STEFANIE:  Howie, I was pretty fat.

*(Beat.)*

HOWIE:  Well. I'm short.

STEFANIE:  No you're not.

HOWIE:  I'm pretty short.

STEFANIE:  I'm pretty tall.

HOWIE:  Yeah you are.

STEFANIE:  I've thought about sawing my feet off and
shove the nubs into heels.

HOWIE:  I've thought about those leg extension proce-
dures that midgets do.

STEFANIE:  You're not a midget.

HOWIE:  Technically no.
It's really expensive actually. I looked into it. Basically
they rip open your legs. Put rods in your bones. Screws.
And they twist and they twist and slowly, SO slowly,
you grow.
I decided not. To do that.

STEFANIE:  I'm glad.

HOWIE:  I'm glad you didn't cut off your feet.

STEFANIE:  Yet.

*(Beat.)*

> I looked for you once on *Facebook* I think but / you're not on

HOWIE:  Yeah I'm not on there.

STEFANIE:  That's weirdly admirable.

HOWIE:  I just don't know if I could take that kind of pressure. All of those friends.

STEFANIE:  They're not really friends.
Yeah but I – tried to find you. Before. I googled you too, I, just curious about what you were up to.

HOWIE:  Oh, um – I've been going by – my middle name actually business wise so – barely a footprint, Howie's just –
Max. Is what I – go by now -

STEFANIE:  Max.

HOWIE:  Yep! Max.

STEFANIE:  'Max.' *(Beat.)* Can I call you Howie still?

HOWIE:  Sure.

STEFANIE:  You can call me Stefanie.

HOWIE:  I will.

STEFANIE:  And we'll say each other's names, and it'll be great.

*(STEFANIE takes a breath, like she's about to announce something or tread new territory –)*

STEFANIE:  So – do you remember when -

*(but ANDY re-approaches, a bit drunker.)*

ANDY:  This is crazy. This is *crazy*. I just talked to this guy who – he was like – remember Brad, he played lacrosse? It was Brad. One time after gym he hit me with his lacrosse stick for like no reason like just for shits? His hairline is rapidly receding and lives with his parents. He lives with his *parents.*

*(raising his glass --)*

To revenge.

HOWIE:  Technically you lived with *your* parent until two years ago.

ANDY:  *(embarrassed)* Yeah I know.

*(ANDY drinks.
ANDY approaches the large framed picture of KEN.)*

ANDY:  You having fun Ken? Can I get you a drink?

HOWIE:  Stop.

ANDY:  He looks bored.

HOWIE:  C'mon Andy – leave him – it -- alone.

ANDY:  Okay - He was a dick to you, How.

HOWIE:  I really don't remember, it probably wasn't --

STEFANIE:  It was. He was.

HOWIE:  Like how? What did he do?

*(MELISSA, again, at the mic.)*

MELISSA (O.S.):  Ohhhhhhhkay!
So now we're going to start the karaoke! So – so there's a songbook here and so you just have to – so write the number of the song on the index card and give it to the DJ and so – who's going to be our first brave soul? Come on don't make me come out there and / select someone OKAY! Wendy! I have Wendy Love or should I say MRS. JED JENNINGS up here to sing a little song for us! Yayyyyyyyy Wendy, takin one for the team!

*(Lights come up on WENDY, totally plastered, on stage with mic.*

*HOWIE, ANDY and STEFANIE turn to her and watch, horrified.)*

WENDY:  What's up Spartans WOOOO!!!!!!!!!!
I'm so happy to see everybody this is so so amazing and I'm going to sing a song from the good ol days so this is like REALLY serious so don't laugh at me or anything cause I can't sing or anything, it's been a while, but I did accapella in college, Lorelei's what's UP, *(singing) OooOOoooooo,* okay so, here I go, okay.

*(WENDY sings very seriously, with much emotion,* No Doubt's *"Don't Speak.")*

WENDY:
> *You and me*
> *We used to be together*
> *Everyday together always*
> *I really feel*
> *That I'm losin my best friend*
> *I can't believe this could be*
> *The end*
> *It looks as though*
> *You're letting go*
> *And if it's real well I don't want to knowwwwww*
> *DON'T SPEAK -*

*(The music suddenly cuts out.)*

VOICE: Sorry – sorry – hold on Wendy sorry –
    Could somebody – could somebody look at the thingy?

WENDY: It's okay – I'm done.

*(Self consciously, she replaces the mike on the stand, and exits.*

*Softly, slowly, the room begins to spin. The evening progresses, passes. Music surges. Nametags fall to the floor. Ties are loosened.*
*Girls grind on each other.*
*The JROTC kids once lining the walls slowly pry themselves away and move towards the tables of cheese.*

*ANDY, JED and HOWIE, an hour later, a bit drunk.)*

JED: So millionaire!

HOWIE: Yep!

JED: I'm impressed.

ANDY: Yeah he's like super / grassroots

JED: So what's your investment portfolio like, what kind / of

HOWIE: Oh I'm not so much into investing yet, just focusing on what I have –

ANDY: I bought some apple stock, yeah, I did it years ago -

HOWIE: You bought like one share.

ANDY: Yeah but –

JED: I'm really lookin to beef up my portfolio man, maybe I'll invest in your company.

HOWIE: Maybe you should!

JED: Maybe I will!

ANDY: Yeah maybe I will too!

*(HOWIE gives him a weird look. Nearly: you're embarrassing me.*
*ANDY is humiliated.)*

ANDY: Yeahhhhh I'm just gonna - go over there now. Cool…….

*(He goes.)*

JED: *(of ANDY)* Is he gay now?

*(HOWIE isn't sure how to answer, then nods.)*

JED: CALLED IT!

*(Beat. Then suddenly: ANDY on the mic.)*

ANDY: What's up you guys I'm going to a do a little the art of song for you right now. Imma take you guys back to high school since we're already there if that's cool….

*(They watch his super ambitious and self conscious if not pretentious performance of "Plush" by Stone Temple Pilots.)*

ANDY: This is a song called Plush.
*AND I FEEL*
*SO MUCH DEPENDS ON THE WEATHER*
*SO IS IT RAINING IN YOUR BEDROOM*
*AND I SEE*
*THAT THESE ARE THE EYES OF DISARRAY*
*WOULD YOU EVEN CARE*
*AND I FEEL IT*
*AND SHE FEELS IT*

Howie do you remember this?! Remember this?!

*WHERE YOU GONE TO TOMMORROW*
*WHERE YOU GONE WITH THE MASK I FOUND*
*AND I FEEL AND WHEN THE DOGS BEGIN TO*
*SMELL HER*
*WILL SHE SMELL ALONE*

*(HOWIE tries to ignore Andy, tries to stand taller. Andy's song fades into the background, as:)*

JED: 'Max.'

HOWIE: Yep!

*(Beat.)*

JED: I drive an Edge.
   It's an SUV Hybrid.

*(JED drinks. HOWIE nods. JED talks to hear himself talk.)*

   Sunroof, beautiful grill in the front, commands attention on the road.
   I don't think too much about what's going on upstairs, whatever crisis is going on, but I mean, I read the news, and I see that Ford was one of the only automotive companies reporting profit this year, *profit,* but I just do my job which is to make whoever walks in my door buy one of those fuckin cars, what do you drive?

HOWIE: I don't have a car.

JED: That's cool, that's cool -

HOWIE: I bike.

JED: Faggot.

*(Howie smiles. JED laughs, then realizes that this is not funny, at all. He drinks.)*

   Ford's got good cars and when I sell a hybrid, I always push hybrids, I feel like I'm doing my part.
   I'm providing for my family and that's – that's what counts, so that's what counts so that's what I do.

*(HOWIE nods, which makes him dizzy.)*

JED: I remember my Mom told me you were doing that, the Peace Corps and stuff.
   That woulda been pretty cool. See the world for free.
   We got down to Florida last year.

*(JED drinks. So does Howie. He looks green.)*

You alright there? You gotta pace yourself, man.

HOWIE: I'm good.

JED: Lightweight, huh?

HOWIE: *(defensively)* No, fuck no. I just don't usually drink, ah. I usually just drink beer I don't drink, ah – whiskey, ah --

JED: You know our moms are friends?
They're still friends, since when we were little.

*(HOWIE nods, remembering something.)*

HOWIE: We were in the back of your Mom's minivan. You and me and Ken. It was burgundy?

JED: Yeah, hell yeah! THE GRAPE MONSTER!

HOWIE: And I was pulling your –
The strings of your hoodie I was pulling them so that the hole closed up over your face and you couldn't breathe but you were laughing, and I was laughing –

JED: She was taking us to see Ghostbusters!!

HOWIE: Yeah and – we got pepperoni personal pan pizzas and – we were singing the fast part of Hook, we knew ever word, and Ken sang it the fastest and the best and
Your mom got mad because I ripped your sweatshirt and –
So She took me home.

*(Beat.)*

Then we stopped hanging out. Then it stopped.

JED: What stopped?

HOWIE: Fifth grade. Right before middle school.
And then it changed.
And Ken changed.

*(JED grows quiet, remembering.)*

JED: He was just messing with you.

HOWIE: But it doesn't matter anymore. I'm different,
I'm –

JED: Yeah.

*(JED is incredibly self conscious.)*

I'm gonna, uh. Grab another beer.

*(JED goes. HOWIE stands alone.*
*The stage behind HOWIE begins to glow.*
*Suddenly, a hot hot sun.*
*HOWIE approaches it. He kicks off his shoes, takes off his*
*shirt, cuffs his pants.*
*The sound of a hundred hungry kids.)*

HOWIE: Mom and Dad, I'm sorry I haven't written yet
but I just now got a chance.
I'm all settled, I wouldn't say 'comfortable' but there's
a weird comfort in the discomfort if that makes any
sense at all.

Argentina is like Arizona, or like what I recall Arizona to be when we went to visit Aunt Jackie.

We're going to be growing vegetables and also building 'fogones.'

Essentially it's an outdoor stove. Here they mostly do their cooking indoors, and their homes if you can even call them homes have little to no ventilation, which causes some pretty serious respiratory issues. With these outdoor stoves they'll be able to avoid this altogether.

*(HOWIE starts to build.)*

JED:  Son it's Dad. You sound happy and smart.
Sounds like your English degree is really coming in handy.
I'm going to put your mom on now.

ANDY:  Sup Howard!! How's Brazil or wherever you are? Where are you even? You gotta get on fuckbook so I can track you like you're my child. Band's picking up, finally got rid a Roger, got a new drummer who does NOT pass out during the set, so things are good, and we got a gig at Piedmont Bowling so I am not suicidal, just suicidal adjacent.

*(Beat.)*

My mom's not doing so well. So there's that.

*(Beat.)*

So that's me.
I miss you, man, wherever you are.
Peace.

STEFANIE:  Hi Howie, this is your mother and I am writing an email your Dad showed me how to write an email and now I am writing it. I hope you are staying nice and warm wait I just 'Googled' Argentina and it is not very cold there so I hope you are staying nice and Cool. Drink lots of water but don't drink from the rivers or any standing water, drink bottled water.

I wanted to tell you some news from home. A boy you went to high school with, Ken Strong, do you remember him? He was in your grade. He was killed in a car accident.

They're saying it had something to do with alcohol it's all very sad.

*(HOWIE hears this. Drops to his knees. Starts to cry. As quickly as the tears starts, he stops them.)*

Okay now I am done with the email so I guess I will say 'bye' and I love you. Get some sleep, don't be crazy.

HOWIE:  Mom:  That's sad but if it's okay, I don't want to hear anything about home. All of my problems or anything I once perceived to be problems now seem incredibly small. I have a new perspective.
Dad I want your advice re: starting a small business. I have an idea for a business.

ANDY:  Hey How / Max / Howard / whatever I'm supposed to call you now, I don't even know if you have internet wherever you are, maybe you don't, but it'd be nice to hear from you. Maybe your address changed but if you get this: Ken Strong is dead. Fuck. I want to go to the funeral but I also do not want to go to the funeral.

In my fantasy life, you email me back and say you're coming home and then we go together to the funeral and then we go to Applebees.

Hope you're good, wherever you are.

…Howie?

How?


MELISSA (O.S.): Okay you guys some fun facts for you guys!

In our graduating class there are 6 marriages! 80% of our graduating class still reside in our hometown! We've got 3 lawyers, 20 nurses, 10 policemen, 23 in the armed forces God Bless you guys and lady, 37 teachers, and 17 unaccounted for!

*(The sun / arid land fade away.*

*HOWIE, back at reunion, standing barefoot. Where are his shoes?*
*JED, ANDY, WENDY and STEFANIE watching.)*

ANDY: How? You okay?

STEFANIE: Howie?

HOWIE: I still feel so – why do I feel so small –

VOICE: Ohhhhh kay we've got a new victim you guys, HOWIE!!!!

HOWIE: What?

ANDY: I signed you up for karaoke.

HOWIE: No – No.

*(Chants begin. HOW-EE. HOW-EE.)*

HOWIE: Why did you do that?

ANDY: What? All eyes on you, no problem, you're a big man now!

*(All eyes are on him, indeed. Mortified, HOWIE goes to the mic.)*

HOWIE: Max. It's Max.

VOICE: Okay – Max – is gonna sing a little song for us, a little –

HOWIE: Hello everyone. I remember you. And you, and you, and you.
What are we doing here? WHAT THE FUCK ARE WE DOING HERE?
WHY ARE WE BACK HERE?
Why does this matter so much?

*(Beat.)*

I just want you all to know I mean you've probably heard now that I'm a millionaire now, and so FUCK YOU ALL!

*(He laughs, strangely.)*

Nice to see you.

*(The music comes on, "Hook" by Blues Traveler, HOWIE starts to sing. Softly. Embarrassed.)*

HOWIE:
*It doesn't matter what I say*
*So long as I sing with inflection*
*That makes you feel I'll convey*

*Some inner truth or vast reflection*
*But I've said nothing so far*
*And I can keep it up for as long as it takes*
*And it don't matter who you are*
*If I'm doing my job then it's your resolve that breaks*

*Because the Hook brings you back*
*I ain't tellin' you no lie*
*The Hook brings you back*
*On that you can rely*

*(During: JED, STEFANIE and WENDY. JED is surveying the crowd.)*

JED: 'snot a great turn out.
Man *everybody* was at mine last year.
Ronnie and Marybeth, Melissa, Joe, Jeff Hummel, Claire and that other one, ALL the freakin ROTC kids, the step team kids, the ones who dressed like their parents, the art girl with the camel toe, they all actually came.

WENDY: *(to JED)* Should we call the sitter, check in?

JED: Called her an hour ago.

WENDY: You didn't tell me, what'd she say?

JED: That she was sleeping.

WENDY: *(to STEFANIE)* Sorry, Mommy talk.
*(To JED)* On her back or her stomach?

JED: I didn't ask.

WENDY: Well if it was her stomach –

JED:  Didn't ask, Wendy.

*(Beat.)*

STEFANIE:  This is so fun!

WENDY:  Can you call her back and ask?

JED:  I just called. An hour ago. Honey –

*(WENDY knows to stop pushing it. They all drink.)*

STEFANIE:  I'm sorry. About Sophia. I'm so so sorry.

*(WENDY is a bit shocked to hear this.*
*JED drinks, looks around the room. Is silent.)*

   I saw –I heard that she --

WENDY:  Oh – well that's – thanks.
   It's really fine actually, we're very blessed, we're really
   hopeful, we won't know for another six months or so
   the extent of – any damage but –

STEFANIE:  I'm so sorry –

WENDY:  Yeah, no, it's totally fine it just –

STEFANIE:  So it was all fine and then / just

WENDY:  Yeah her umbilical cord, um. And so she did-
   n't have *air* for like –

JED:  *(please stop)* Is that Mr. Gaither?

WENDY: She has the most amazing smile –and her spirit – she just really warms my heart, it's crazy, I think of her, and I melt completely. *(Tears come to her eyes.)* Like right now. It's happening right now.
And Jed – Jed's such a good Daddy.

JED: *(forcing a smile)* Yep, that's me.

STEFANIE: They say – they say that kids like this are born for a reason.

JED: *(hard)* Like what? Like what reason?

STEFANIE: Well you know they um – they bring light to people's lives –

*(JED downs his drink. Goes.)*

WENDY: Where're you going?

JED: To the fucking bathroom, Wendy.
I'll be right back, I gotta piss, you wanna come? You wanna watch?

WENDY: Call – I'll call the babysitter –

*(WENDY and STEFANIE, alone.)*

STEFANIE: Where'd Howie go?

*(WENDY shrugs.)*

WENDY: Poor little guy.

STEFANIE: He's / not little

WENDY: I keep thinking I'm almost going to puke but then not puking. Ha!

(STEFANIE nods. WENDY looks like she might cry, but fights it.)

WENDY: I barely know anybody anymore, it's so weird! I used to know everybody.

(Beat.)

It was weird, I thought I'd be a big part of the planning committee, I mean, and then I ran into Melissa at Marshall's and they'd already started planning it and I was like, I can help, so……

(She trails off. She retrieves her camera from her purse and obsessively takes pictures with her camera of everyone, everything.)

WENDY: Takeesha! Molly! Get together! Yeah, get to together! Molly, put your arm around Takeesha!

(WENDY takes a picture.)

Yayyyy!

(WENDY looks around nervously for other pictures to take.)

Now one of you!

(STEFANIE poses weirdly.)

WENDY: Beautiful!!

*(WENDY takes the picture.)*

You wanna see?

*(STEFANIE looks.)*

STEFANIE: Meh.

WENDY: You look *amazing.*

STEFANIE: Thanks.

WENDY: No seriously I was over at the yearbooks and I was like, me and Jenny Goodman were like, We were looking at your picture and she was like that girl is *here* and I was like no she's *not* because Stefanie I seriously did not recognize you, you are the MOST you look SO much better you look SO good.

*(She drinks.)*

STEFANIE: You look great too!

WENDY: Sophia made me fat.

*(Beat.)*

Jed – um – he's just – it's really hard for him?

STEFANIE: Yeah -

WENDY: And you try not to be but it's like *why, why* is this happening to us, you know?!

STEFANIE: I think I know why.

WENDY: You do?

STEFANIE:  She's made you sweet.
   I'm just saying there is now a – sweetness. To you.
   That wasn't there before, so. Back then.
   Maybe that's why.

*(WENDY nods, dries her eyes.)*

WENDY:  Were we friends?

STEFANIE:  Um --?

WENDY:  I can't remember if we were friends, I can't
   remember –

STEFANIE:  Not so much.

WENDY:  Was I – not sweet to you?

STEFANIE:  It doesn't matter. We're friends now, right?

WENDY:  We need a picture of us.

STEFANIE:  Yeah, okay!

*(WENDY takes their picture, their faces smushed together
like friends.
WENDY hugs her, desperately. They hug and hug.
WENDY sees someone.)*

WENDY:  Melissa! Hey Melissa!

*(Wendy separates, dropping Stefanie as if she were hot.)*

STEFANIE:  Well it's nice / to --

*(WENDY leaves STEFANIE alone without saying bye.)*

STEFANIE: See you. Now.

*(STEFANIE stands alone. At first she's pissed, then sad, and then she realizes there's just no point. In a tiny moment, she grows up. Moves on.*

*Then: The music seems to get louder. And louder.*
*Two of the JROTC girls are making out.*
*A husband screams through the phone at the babysitter.*
*A cheerleader tries to call a cab but pukes instead.*
*A group of football players, now fat, eat cake and drink warm beer.*
*ANDY finds HOWIE.*
*HOWIE is pretty drunk.*
*He fishes for his phone. Checks it.)*

ANDY: Howie. Stop.

HOWIE: I'm just fuckin lookin at my phone.

*(Beat.)*

She said she 'couldn't get over our height difference.' Four years. 'Couldn't get over our height difference.'

ANDY: Well – that's bullshit.

HOWIE: Is it?

*(Beat.)*

ANDY: Fuck her, you're a *millionaire,* you're gonna get a pool and empty it out and Duck Tales the shit out of that pool!

HOWIE: *(shaking his head)* I told her – I told her about the money, I told her – I'd take care of her, I'd pay her loans, I'd buy her a pony, a castle, a castle pony, all of the fucking purses, show her the whole world, if she would just – love me, keep loving me, but – it wasn't enough.

ANDY: She sucked anyways.

HOWIE: What?

ANDY: Rachel. Sucked. And she made you suck. She made you like - not yourself. She made you try way too hard. You shouldn't have to try so hard.

HOWIE: I'm not trying hard –

ANDY: Tell that to your blazer dude.

HOWIE: Please stop. Please please stop.

*(Beat.)*

ANDY: Fine.

*(Beat.)*

It's weird to be back home.

*(Howie laughs, just a little.)*

ANDY: What?

*(Beat.)*

HOWIE: You're not 'back.'
You only moved half an hour away.

ANDY:  Yeah but I don't live *here* anymore.

*(HOWIE smiles wryly.)*

ANDY:  …What?

HOWIE:  Nothing.

ANDY:  ….I don't live here anymore.

HOWIE:  Remember when I beat you to the knot badge and you got so mad? Because I beat you?

ANDY:  Why're / you

HOWIE:  You got SO. MAD.

*(HOWIE laughs.)*

And remember when Ken was like, we were camping we were like ten and he was like: I want to kill a rabbit. I want to kill and skin a rabbit and we were like, *whatttt????*

*(HOWIE laughs and laughs.)*

I have a boat.
I have a really big boat.
*(at his drink)* Need a refill.

ANDY:  You're wasted –

HOWIE:  I'm good.

ANDY:  ….I don't live here anymore.
YES it's only 26 miles but do you know, do you know how hard it was, for me to make it out of my fucking driveway? Leave my Mom even for 26 miles?

*(Beat.*

*JED passes, raising a glass to HOWIE.)*

JED:  LITTLE MAN!!!!!!!

*(HOWIE closes his eyes. JED passes.)*

ANDY:  We don't have to be here. We can go.

HOWIE:  This is so great! To see everybody!

*(Beat.)*

ANDY:  You're kidding right?

HOWIE:  I'm staying! This is happening.

*(Beat.)*

ANDY:  You're not even –

HOWIE:  What?

ANDY:  You're not even like – you're pretending like
    nothing bad happened. At all. That doesn't count.

*(Beat.)*

HOWIE:  I'm sorry you had a tough time then but –

ANDY:  SO DID YOU.

*(Beat.)*

HOWIE:  I have a boat.

ANDY: It doesn't count if you pretend it didn't happen, that doesn't count.

HOWIE: You're making a REALLY big deal out of NOTHING it was NOTHING

ANDY: Oh, okay, whatever.

HOWIE: I'm sorry if you have a problem with these people but I'm having a nice time.

ANDY: You think you can just show up here and have it all just be / like

HOWIE: Do you have a boat?

ANDY: I'm a musician, I have no need for a boat.

HOWIE: *(under his breath)* Do you get paid to make music?

ANDY: What?

HOWIE: Do you get paid?

*(Beat. ANDY, hurt.)*

ANDY: Wow. That's – really -

*(ANDY downs his drink, goes.)*

ANDY: I'm um –

HOWIE: It was a logistical question, I was just / wondering if

ANDY:  I've never made you feel small, man. Not on pur-
pose.
Not when everybody made fun of you.
Not when Ken / made your

HOWIE:  Don't say it I don't wanna talk about it can we
just

ANDY:  I'm gonna go, you can stay if you want, I just –

HOWIE:  Andy –

ANDY:  No, I'm out.

*(ANDY goes. HOWIE stands alone, exposed.*

*JED, on the mic.)*

JED:  Dude I want a duet right now!
I want Little Man to join me up on this stage for a
DUET! Where'd he go?

*(Chanting again. LITTLE MAN. LITTLE MAN. LITTLE
MAN.*

*HOWIE takes the picture of KEN STRONG, and goes.*

*He passes by WENDY who sits at a table by herself. She's
tired, drunk, and is looking at the pictures on her camera
over and over.*

*JED leaves the mike and approaches her, slowly.*

*He sits next to her.)*

WENDY:  I got a lot of pictures. I got so many pictures.

JED:  Good.

*(Beat.)*

WENDY:  What happened to us?

JED:  How do you mean?

WENDY:  We used to be – so –

*(Beat.)*

Are we sad?

JED:  No –

WENDY:  Do you promise?

JED:  I'm not sad.

*(Beat.)*

WENDY:  What if Sophia – what if she can never talk or
walk or

JED:  She'll be fine.

WENDY:  But we don't know that.

JED:  Can we do this at home?

WENDY:  No, I wanna talk about this, I'm tired of not
talking about this!

JED:  We can talk about this. At home.

WENDY:  We're not leaving yet, nobody's left yet, we can't be the first to leave!

JED:  These aren't even my people.

WENDY:  *I'm* your people.

*(Beat.)*

JED:  Everything's backwards.

WENDY:  But it's gonna be okay, right? Even if it's not exactly like we – it's gonna be okay?

JED:  Yeah.

WENDY:  How do you know?

JED:  I don't, I'm just real good at lying to myself.

WENDY:  I wanna be good at that.

JED:  No you don't.

*(He puts his head in his hands.)*

Millionaire.

WENDY:  What?

JED:  I'm an asshole, I can't do anything right, I can't even make a kid right –

WENDY:  Aw, sweetie, no no no, c'mere –

*(They hold each other. Genuinely, for a good moment. They really do love each other and we see this clearly here.)*

WENDY: You want some water?

*(JED nods.)*

I'll get you some water.

*(WENDY puts a hand on JED's shoulder, just for a moment, as she leaves.*
*JED, alone.*
*HOWIE, wasted, sitting against his old locker. Sitting next to him is the framed portrait of Ken. He's got his arm around it. He's trying to call ANDY.)*

HOWIE: *(to portrait)* It's ringing.

*(HOWIE waits.)*

He's not answering.
Andy.
This is my last and final message so this is really serious right now.

*(Beat.)*

You're right this is WEIRD. This whole thing. This is so WEIRD right now. I'm sitting outside Mr. Spangler's room with my old buddy Ken and I can hear – our voices -
Where are you did you go to Applebees without me?
Did you get a booth? Are you in our booth?
I'd totally come meet you man but I'm kinda – I'm kinda drunk and I –

*(Beat.)*

I'm sorry. I didn't mean to like –that's not what I meant.

Your mom's real lucky to have you.
You know what I don't know if I could do that. What you've done. For your Mom. I mean when my Dad lost his job and my mom was going nuts and everything I didn't – I didn't even come home. I just bought them a house. But that's not the same. As what you've done. Please man. Please call me back.

*(Beat.)*

When Ken – when he made me cry, and –

*(HOWIE sucks back tears.)*

And you came over and we microwaved nacho's and you just sat with me and we didn't talk about it and I really appreciate that. I remember that. I really –
Please Andy. Please call me back.

*(Beat.)*

I'll buy you a boat. I'll –

RECORDING: If you are satisfied with your message / please

HOWIE: *Fuckkkkkkkkkkkk*

*(HOWIE throws his phone. Just sits there.*

*He speaks softly to the portrait.)*

Heyyyyyyy buddy.
Hey Ken. Kenneth.
Kenneth Nicholas Strong.
What's up.

What's up buddy.
How's it going?

*(Beat.)*

Me? I'm fine.
How's hell? Are you on fire a little bit? That sucks.
I tried to tell you that there was really a heaven and a hell but you didn't listen.
Granted you were like 10.
Sorry you died.
Did it hurt?

*(Beat.)*

They say you were wasted which I don't find surprising.
Your body wrapped around that tree and you bled Miller Light. Sorry about your car.
You know what's funny though is that *you* died and *I* lived. I am alive right now. Sort of.
But lemmee – lemmee get philosophical for like JUST a minute okay? AM I really alive? Am I really living or am I somehow stuck in these halls trying to duck every time you come at me? Thinking of things I coulda said to you to get you to stop.
Pussy.
Pussy.
You fucking PUSSY.

*(Beat. HOWIE starts to beat and kick the portrait.)*

YOU. MOTHER. FUCKING. HORRIBLE. HEARTLESS. LITTLE. BITCH.
YOU TINY FUCKING PIECE OF SHIT!!!!!

YOU ARE SMALL!! TOUCH ME AGAIN AND I'LL KILL YOU, PUSSY, I'LL KILL YOU AND YOUR SISTER AND YOUR CAR!!!!!
YOU. TINY LITTLE PIECE. OF. SHIT.

*(Beat. HOWIE breathes heavy. Sees the damage he's done.*
*HOWIE, for the first time, really processes that KEN is dead. He sits there processing this.)*

I have a boat.

*(Beat.*

*HOWIE sits next to the portrait.*

*STEFANIE approaches.)*

STEFANIE:  Are you okay?

*(HOWIE stirs.)*

HOWIE:  I can taste my hangover.

STEFANIE:  What's it like.

HOWIE:  Gasoline and toast.

STEFANIE:  Yum.

HOWIE:  This was my locker.

*(STEFANIE looks up.)*

STEFANIE:  Good memory.
     *(Of portrait:)* What happened here?

HOWIE: Feelings.

STEFANIE: Ah.
   I won't tell.

*(Beat.)*

HOWIE: I – had forgotten all about – all of this. All the
   shit that happened here. I tried to tell myself it never
   happened and then I think I actually forgot it.

STEFANIE: I remember every second.

HOWIE: You do?

STEFANIE: It's a gift and also a curse.

HOWIE: For me it's so – fuzzy I had like – packed it
   away beneath ALL my winter sweaters and ALL the
   *Lands End* turtle necks my Mom bought me and – but
   now I remember.
   Because so many times I cried in my car.

STEFANIE: Me too.

HOWIE: I was crying in my car and it was raining so
   hard I was hoping – no one could see into my car but –
   he saw me crying in my car.
   That was the worst.
   Because I could see that he felt bad. That he didn't
   know, he thought he was being funny, I don't know,
   because of something his mom did, something his Dad
   didn't do, why do we ever do anything?

STEFANIE: Unrequited needs from middle school, that's
   why I slept with anyone / who'd look at me, anyone
   who looked at me

HOWIE:  And it's so – it's so – I think about it and I
   *shrivel up* I
   You're – you look very nice by the way.

STEFANIE:  He was an asshole.
   Thank you.

HOWIE:  Wasn't everybody?

STEFANIE:  You weren't. *(Beat.)* It's all over now.

HOWIE:  Is it?

STEFANIE:  Sort of.

HOWIE:  I want it to really be over. *Really.*

STEFANIE:  If you say it is, then it is.

HOWIE:  How?

STEFANIE:  Say 'it's over.'

HOWIE:  'It's over.'

STEFANIE:  Say 'I am better than these people now.'

HOWIE:  'I am –' am I?

STEFANIE:  We are. *(Beat.)* I think that's why I came?

HOWIE:  Why?

STEFANIE:  To prove that, to myself?

HOWIE:  Me too.

STEFANIE:  I just had one of those 'bathroom epipha-
nies' about it.

*(Beat.)*

HOWIE:  Andy's – Andy's a good guy. He'll –
I'll buy him a doughnut. I'll –
*(Beat.)*
He thinks *I* think I'm better than him, he thinks, but
that's – that's *crazy.* *(Beat.)* That's *crazy.*

*(HOWIE sits, knowing that its true, that he thinks that.)*

STEFANIE:  Howie?

HOWIE:  Yes, tuba?

STEFANIE:  I, um.
I have to tell you. I don't want you to think that I'm just
saying this because – just know that I'm genuinely saying this.

HOWIE:  Okay?

STEFANIE:  I had – the *biggest* crush on you then.

HOWIE:  Wait, seriously?

STEFANIE:  *So* bad.

HOWIE:  This is amazing!
Someone had a crush on me! I wish I'da known, I
woulda ruled that lunch room, man.

STEFANIE:  I don't think me having a crush on you
woulda carried much weight.

HOWIE: We could've sat together.

STEFANIE: I would've eaten your lunch.

HOWIE: So what you wanted to like put me in a pocket, or on a shelf? I'm familiar –

STEFANIE: No I like – really liked you. I wrote you *poems* I have *journals* from Hot Topic filled with *poems*.

HOWIE: Do you have any memorized?

STEFANIE: Ha! No.

*(Beat.*

*Then, quickly:)*

> I smell you well
> From 3 doors down
> Fragrance cloaks / me

HOWIE: Wait, what?

STEFANIE: Shhhhh this is a poem. Oh my God, I'm saying this right now!
Okay.

HOWIE: *(reverently)* Okay, Okay –

STEFANIE: 'Looks me round.
So familiar, I've smelled it before. The vibes make me sick as I level the floor.
So sweet, I enjoy it
So dizzy, I fall
The scent of your presence:
The bottle is small.

*(HOWIE starts to clap, genuinely touched.)*

HOWIE:  Wow – *wow* –

STEFANIE:  Thank you, thank you, that one was my favorite.

HOWIE:  Wait, I smelled?

STEFANIE:  Like – um.
Like cinnamon and dryer sheets. And *Pop Tarts,* but just a little bit.

*(Beat.)*

HOWIE:  Why didn't you say anything?

*(Beat.)*

STEFANIE:  One time – you came over to my house to practice -

HOWIE:  Wait - Yes! I remember this!

STEFANIE:  And it was so, *so* awkward because my Mom wasn't wearing a bra, / huge boobs

HOWIE:  *Huge* boobs

STEFANIE:  Yeah and she kept trying to give us snack cakes, she kept saying 'snack cake.'

HOWIE:  Yeah it was those little Christmas trees!

STEFANIE:  But it was March.

HOWIE:  I ate one.

STEFANIE:  I ate four. And then after we practiced you – *lingered,* you didn't leave, and – we watched The Cosby show -

HOWIE:  *(remembering)* You were comforting.

STEFANIE:  Fat.

HOWIE:  No I was – sitting next to you on that couch, we were kind of close together, yeah and I thought: my room at home. I shut the door and I breathe out and I lock it *and I'm completely safe and my bed's warm and I can sleep for days.*

*(Beat. STEFANIE exhales.)*

STEFANIE:  And I called you later that night but you weren't there you were / playing

HOWIE:  D&D most likely

STEFANIE:  And I told your Mom to tell you I'd called and you didn't call me back.

*(Beat.)*

HOWIE:  She didn't tell me.

STEFANIE:  She didn't?

HOWIE:  Definitely not.

STEFANIE:  You're just saying that!

HOWIE:  No seriously she didn't tell me!

STEFANIE:  Oh, okay.

*(STEFANIE slips off her shoes. They sit there for quite some time.)*

MELISSA (O.S.): Whooooooooooo okay you guys, okay okay it's gettin *late* what WHAT!
Okay so first could whoever took Ken's portrait please return it because that's seriously not cool okay? Okay. I'm serious.

Ummmmmmmm okay so announcements somebody's lights are on. Somebody's light's are on, I've got it – right here – okay it's a Wrangler. It's a 2005 *Wrangler.* And your lights are ON. And PLEASE don't use the lil boys room because it's flooding.

Okay and so in like half an hour they're gonna have to kick us out of here but you guys the night has just BE-GUN! We're gonna have some cabs meet us outside and take us to the AFTER PARTY!

I'm sure you've still got lots of catching up to do and I haven't even gotten to talk to like half of you guys yet so let's keep it going, whooooooo!!!!!!!

*(STEFANIE lays her head on HOWIE's shoulder.)*

Because you know what guys? This night is just too good to end.
It's the party we totally deserve for growing up!
It's a big pat on the back. Some of us have jobs. Some of us even have kids and health insurance. I have a Wii and a Pomerianian and my parents haven't paid my rent in six months.

*(The voice now seems to get farther and farther away, as does the music.)*

Some of us have driveways and accountants and cabinets full of suppressed trauma and yearbooks. I have a Tupperware set from Target. We are grown ups now and we only drink five nights a week and never past midnight, nothing a Gatorade and a breakfast burrito can't cure. We keep abortions to a minimum, we keep it classy.

Yesterday I ran two miles. When I go home to my parents house I put on my old cheerleading uniform and lay next to a younger version of myself and when I sleep she whispers in my ear, over and over, *you are so awesome. You are still so awesome.* And I only cry a little bit but it's only because I'm happy.

And we *are* awesome.

Let's make tonight last forever and ever.

And ever and ever.

*(Beat.)*

And ever and ever and ever.

And ever and ever.

HOWIE: Down here we're the same height.

*(STEFANIE smiles.*

*Lights.)*

END OF PLAY.

## More Plays From
## Bekah Brunstetter

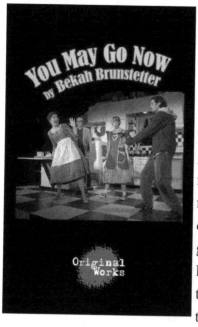

**YOU MAY GO NOW**

**Synopsis:** Dottie has trained young Betty to be the perfect 1950s housewife; to cook the perfect pot roast, to bake a gorgeous seven-layer cake, to remove any stain. And tonight, Betty's 18th birthday, it is time for Betty to go out into the world. Only Dottie has failed to mention that it is now the 21st Century, that the world is a vast and complex place, and that there is a reason she cannot abide being called 'Mother'. Ghosts from the past haunt the women and shatter their idyllic, if odd, existence. When a mysterious traveler is stranded at their home, he brings a revelation that forces Betty to choose between the love of her 'mother' and her freedom and sanity. YOU MAY GO NOW is an adult fairy tale about a 'mother' and 'daughter' whose love is as real as it is destructive.

**Cast Size:** 2 Males, 2 Females

## ROBERTA LAUGHS

**Synopsis:** Roger doesn't know his Grandma Roberta very well - but he knows she's "wicked awesome." In an effort to impress the girls at school he's decided to take up the accordion, just as his Grandma played when she was his age. But when the fiercely independent Roberta suffers a debilitating stroke and is close to death - Roger takes action to know her better, even if it means getting to know her "boyfriend" Billy too.

**Cast Size:** 1 Senior Male, 1 Senior Female, 1 Teen Male

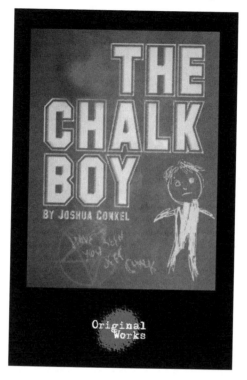

## THE CHALK BOY by Joshua Conkel

**Synopsis:** Beneath its boring facade there is more going on in the tiny town of Clear Creek than the opening of the new Taco Bell. Four of the town's local girls are here to take you on a tour of their funny, yet brutal reality. They struggle with faith, friendship, sex, the occult, algebra, and the disappearance of... The Chalk Boy. This is a deathly black comedy that punches as hard as your high school bully.

**Cast Size:** 4 Females

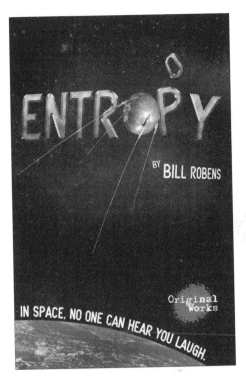

## ENTROPY by Bill Robens

**Synopsis:** With the space race in high gear, and Cold War paranoia at its peak, NASA launches the groundbreaking Zeus rocket on a trip to the Moon, or so they want you to believe. In reality, their mission is to confront and turn newly sentient Soviet satellite, Sputnik, to the cause of freedom. This retro sci-fi parody is filled with zero gravity fun. Strap in and enjoy the ride.

**Cast Size:** Ensemble Cast of 13

## **HARRY AND THE THIEF** by Sigrid Gilmer

**Synopsis:** Mimi's cousin Jeremy has a PhD in physics, a brand new time machine and a plan. He's sending Mimi, a professional thief, back to 1863 to change history by providing Harriet Tubman with modern day guns. Lots and lots of guns.

**Cast Size:** Diverse Cast of 10 Actors

Julianne Homokay's

HUMAN

JUDY GRAY

BIRD

Original Works

## JUDY GRAY
### by Julianne Homokay

**Synopsis:** Judy wants to fly. Judy has wanted to fly as long as she can remember. So, as a vengeful response to her well-meaning yet domineering father, Judy steals his golf clubs and builds her dream wings out of them. Adolescence soon interferes with her goal. Egged on by her Girls in Gray, the relentless inner voices that seek to drive teen-aged girls to destruction, Judy loses sight of herself and lets her attraction to her feather pusher, Birdman, lead her into addiction and promiscuity. In this sense, quirky Judy, with her thick glasses and command of geometry theorems, becomes an Everygirl who must figure out how to grow up in a household that refuses to allow her the room to grow.

**Cast Size:** 2 Males, 8 Females

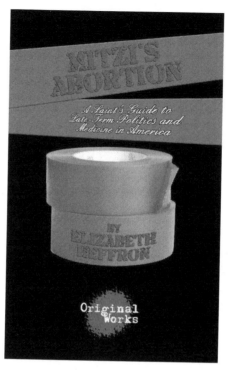

**MITZI'S ABORTION** by Elizabeth Heffron

**Synopsis:** With humor, intelligence and honesty, "Mitzi's Abortion" explores the questions that have shaped the national debate over abortion, and reminds us that whatever we may think we believe, some decisions are neither easy nor simple when they become ours to make. A generous and compassionate comedy with serious themes about a young woman trying to make an intensely personal decision in a system determined to make it a political one.

**Cast Size:** 3 Females, 4 Males

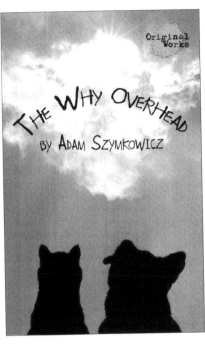

## THE WHY OVERHEAD
### by Adam Szymkowicz

**Synopsis:** At the call center, all are desperate to connect with each other, seek greater meaning and take their desires to extremes. Sam is in love with Violet, a customer who called once with a warranty question, and he smashes all barriers to r e n d e z v o u s  w i t h her. Alan and Sid are blinded in their rivalry for Jessica and together, build a decorative glass window over her cubicle to worship her under. Annie and Nigel have a hate-hate relationship and are each plotting the other's demise. Karen, the department head, plays hooky and makes plans with her sometimes talkative dog to leave the working world entirely in favor of the hobo life. Donald is home too, plotting revenge for being canned as office manager. In the end, the CEO, Mr. Henderson, will sweep in and make everything right, because that's what CEO's do, right?

**Cast Size:** 7 Males, 5 Females

# NOTES

# NOTES

83534560R00058

Made in the USA
San Bernardino, CA
26 July 2018